by Tom Clark

Airplanes (1966)
The Sandburg (1966)
Emperor of the Animals (1967)
Stones (1969)
Air (1970)
Neil Young (1971)
The No Book (1971)
Green (1971)
Smack (1972)
John's Heart (1972)
Blue (1974)
At Malibu (1975)
Fan Poems (1976)
Baseball (1976)
Champagne and Baloney (1976)
35 (1976)
No Big Deal (1977)
How I Broke In (1977)
The Mutabilitie of the Englishe Lyrick (1978)
When Things Get Tough on Easy Street: Selected Poems
    1963–1978 (1978)
The World of Damon Runyon (1978)
One Last Round for The Shuffler (1979)
Who Is Sylvia? (1979)
The Great Naropa Poetry Wars (1980)
The Last Gas Station and Other Stories (1980)
The End of the Line (1980)
A Short Guide to the High Plains (1981)
Heartbreak Hotel (1981)
The Rodent Who Came To Dinner (1981)
Journey to the Ulterior (1981)
Nine Songs (1981)
Under the Fortune Palms (1982)
Dark As Day (1983)
Paradise Resisted: Selected Poems 1978–1984 (1984)
Property (1984)
The Border (1985)
Late Returns: A Memoir of Ted Berrigan (1985)
His Supposition (1986)
Kerouac's Last Word (1986)
The Exile of Céline (1987)
Disordered Ideas (1987)
Apocalyptic Talkshow (1987)
Easter Sunday (1988)
Jack Kerouac in San Francisco (1989)
The Poetry Beat: Reviewing the Eighties (1990)
Fractured Karma (1990)
Charles Olson: The Allegory of a Poet's Life (1991)
Sleepwalker's Fate: New and Selected Poems 1965–1991 (1992)

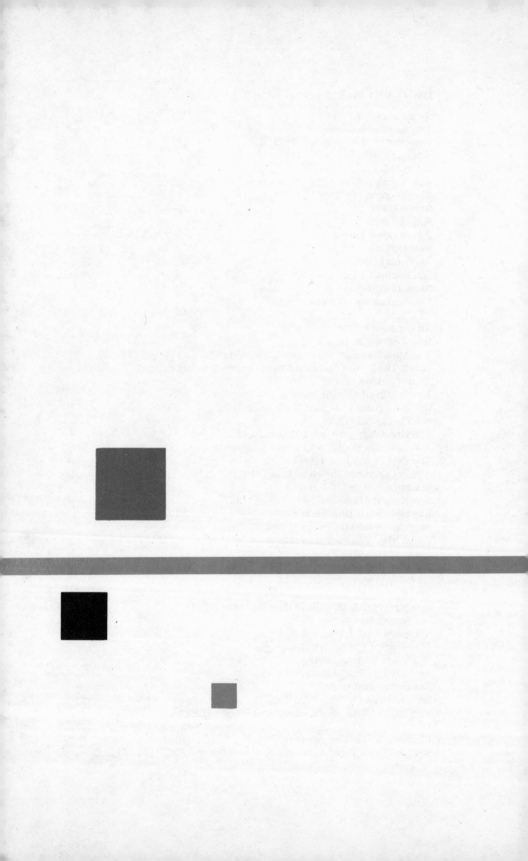

TOM CLARK

SLEEPWALKER'S FATE NEW AND SELECTED POEMS 1965 - 1991

BLACK SPARROW PRESS
SANTA ROSA — 1992

ACKNOWLEDGEMENTS

Some of the new poems first appeared in the following publications: *Blind Date, Brooklyn Review, City Lights Review, Conjunctions, Cover, Die Young, Exquisite Corpse, Gas, Giants Play Well In The Drizzle, Intent, Long News: In the Short Century, New American Writing, Poetry Flash, Prosodia, Santa Monica Review, Scarlet, Shiny, The American Poetry Review, The World,* and *What!*

Most of the poems in the "Dark Continent" section of the book are taken from the volume *When Things Get Tough on Easy Street: Selected Poems 1963–1978* originally published in 1978 and now out of print.

Black Sparrow Press books are printed on acid-free paper.

LIBRARY OF CONGRESS CATALOGING-IN-PUBLICATION DATA

Clark, Tom, 1941–
    Sleepwalker's fate: new and selected poems, 1965-1991 / Tom Clark.
        p.   cm.
    ISBN 0-87685-869-8 (pbk.) : — ISBN 0-87685-870-1 (cloth)
: — ISBN 0-87685-871-X (cloth signed) :
    I. Title.
PS3553.L29S56   1992
811'.54—dc20
                                                    92-4317
                                                      CIP

To Angelica

In walks Krishna's sister with eyes

As a paper card bearing the image of the Patriarca family's patron saint was burned in Floramo's cupped hands, he swore, in Italian, "as burns this saint, so will I burn my soul. I enter alive and I will have to get out dead."

"Come in alive and go out dead," one of the mobsters assembled around Floramo interjected.

—*news account of Mafia initiation rite*

The man who cannot sleep, and I have had only too many occasions for some months to establish the point for myself, refuses more or less consciously to entrust himself to the flow of things.

—*Marguerite Yourcenar*

If you walk in your sleep, forget where you came.

—*Little Milton*

Table of Contents

Sleepwalker's Fate (new poems)

Antiquarian

As the Human Village Prepares for Its Fate 17
Sedge 18
Woodtime 19
The Lyric 20
Statue 21
The Angel's Choice 22
Millennial Icon 24
"Because they are desiring . . ." 25
"A point is fixed . . ." 26
"In this river . . ." 27
Bathed 28
Nodding 29
"Before dawn . . ." 30
Sleepwalker's Way 31
Aubade 32
Somnambulism 33
Calling Infinity 34
Energy of the Pre-World as a Bungee Cable
    Jumper 35
The Pharoahs Sacrifice Themselves Before Her 36
Time 37
Retro 38
Antiquarian 40

Night Patrol

Out of Darkness I Came 43
"Himself let him unknown contain" 44
"The enforced lapse . . ." (Marguerite
    Yourcenar) 45
Spiritual 48

Fate   49
Moira   50
Moira's Messages   51
The Moirai   52
Fate Spinners in Time-Editing Studio, Eternity
    Blvd., 2 A.M.   53
Baby Book Fate Dream   54
The Domestic Life of Ghosts   55
Moodsville   56
A Garland of Red   57
Rojo   58
Or   59
Motion, 1953   60
Coral   61
Theatre   62
Mist Sleeve Flight   63
On Marine Silence Street   64
My Hypertrophic Devotion   65
Personal Angel Glimpsed   66
Ace of Destiny   67
Egypt, Everything   68
Culebra Cascabel   69
Autorotation without Gravity   70
Night Patrol   71

Human Life

Withdrawal   75
A Theory of the Universe   76
Narcissism   77
Human Life   78
West of Eden   79
October   80
"Walked into state . . ."   81
Ancestors   82
1968   83

Terminator Too   84
Sounding Chinese at Inspiration Point   86
Day Detail—Low Light of Afternoon   87
The Silence of the Lambs   88
In the Dark Mountains, Brilliant   90
Fireflies   91
After the Fire—The Woman   92
"First cold winter twilights . . ."   93
De Ira Dei   94
Trout Kill on the Sacramento   95
Milky Turquoise Cloud   96
"In the bond scandals . . ."   97
Sleepwalker   98
Sleepwalker's Fate   99
The Door Gunner to the Moment (A Shau
    Valley 1968)   100
Eternity   101
The Commanders   102
40 Days   103
Desert Wars   105
Daring to Be the Same   106

Diary of Desert War (1990–1991)   109

Dark Continent (1965–1986)

The Lake   157
I'm on an Island   158
Easter Sunday   159
Dark Continent   160
Momentum   161
Change   162
Afternoons   163
Superballs   164
You (V) (after Hölderlin)   165
"Like musical intruments . . ."   167

Love (after La Rochefoucauld)   168
The Last Poem (after Robert Desnos)   169
I Was Born to Speak Your Name   170
"My heart in pieces . . ."   172
Now She Dwells Here   173
Things about You   174
Up in Here   176
One   177
Ah—There   178
Pillow   179
Nimble Rays of Day Bring Oxygen to Her
      Blood   180
Air   181
Every Day   182
Crisis on the Savannah   183
Gift of Tongue   184
Life Notes   185
Whistle Buoy   186
The Door to the Forest   187
Slow Life   188
Birds   189
Crows   190
Sky   191
Eos   192
"The sun shoots high . . ."   193
The Greeks   194
Magic Arrival No. 7   195
The Tire   196
from Suite   197
Radio   201
A Difference   205
Baseball and Classicism   206
Clemente (1934–1972)   207
The Color of Stepped on Gum   208
Realism   209
The Song of the Drowned Ghost in the Pool   210
The Blue Dress   211
Final Farewell   212

Sleepwalker's Fate

(new poems)

Antiquarian

As the Human Village Prepares for Its Fate

While everything external
dies away in the far off
echo of the soul
         still there's a mill wheel turning
it is like a good
kind of tiredness in
the moment before sleep
         by some distant stream
a note of peace
in a life which
will never be peaceful
         as the daylight fades
the dream disintegrates
but the shadow holds
no power
         over what's about to happen

Sedge

Lorelei with wet hair riverine,
black delta, white beaches
coming out of her moonlight shower—
her cold, cold beauty is the chimerical
other for whom the subject's
erotic longing is like a phantom itch
in a part of the body that died long, long
before we started to patrol this part of the river.
Dark eyes, and wet hair trailing in
the reeds like a subjective language of sedge
through which the divine current snakes.

Woodtime

This woman light screened through
these scattered sibyl's leaves
out of which green fancy weaves lawn
sleeves for providential time filters

to cover Mr. Marvel's dainty arms
into human time a time from elsewhere moves
light filtered through inevitable greens
in the violence of Mr. Marvel's woodtime

where he threw his symbolic lamp
over the book of nature entirely
unseen forms emerge from the shade
of forms that are seen but forgotten

The Lyric

Suffering
lament, sorrow and wild
joy commingle in

the lyric—a collective
sigh of relief comes cascading
out of the blue—

a yearning to submerge
in life like the swimmer
in the pool forgetful

immersed and quenched—
water trailing scattered
diamonds in a rustling

voice of resigned subsidence
as though in the same stroke
everyone alive were speaking through you—

Statue

The angel asked, as his shoulders were pressed into the stone
Why me? And taken away from the inhabited body,
Like the lyric voice rustling from memory forests,
Childhood rushes toward death, a wind in those woods,
Crashing through trees, dying out,
Settling like a white mist over everything.

The Angel's Choice

The angel's choice in
Wings of Desire, to

forsake the thin air
and cool distances

of the infinite,
take the plunge into

swirling flesh currents
of drive and fate and

language, wash up a
puzzled nomad sprawled

in wonderment on
bleakly literal

creation shore—
stranded, lost, dense, awed,

awkward, desiring—
feeling sun on one's

skin in the biting
chill of the ruined

city, sensing thirst,
sipping coffee for

the first time, seeing
the color blue for the

first time, kicking feet
in loose dirt, weeping—

all the sad crazy
delicious human

conditional
things—after the vast

nothingness of all
eternity, to

be fledged in this sweet
aching knowledge is

at last truly *something*.

Millennial Icon

(Paul Klee, *Novus Angelus*)

Cut off from the great rebus of stars,
The angel who is blown out
Of heaven on a violent tailwind

Flung from the exploding
Phenomenal storm of signs,
Freefalling in the aftermath

Of the expanding shock wave
Created by the collapse
Of the chaos of drive into meaning,

Faced with the panic prospect
Of a galaxy of language debris
Into which he is headed, a hail

Of memory showering around him,
Looks neither forward nor back but merely
Rolls his eyes as he lapses into

An inverted semiautomatism in
Which the mind figures without
Really being used, like heraldry on

Forever folded wings

"Because they are desiring . . ."

Because they are desiring,
desirable, mortal, and

death-bearing, persons must,
like in manic 50s

tv gameshow gauntlet,
flee in and out of uncanny

state of strangeness, changing
direction compulsively as

drives are triggered and fade
according to readout of

current surge lapsing
back again into inertia,

momentum sustained
as positive charge that

sparks up red shocks, pulsing
across the calm grey green

display window in constantly
shifting systolic waves

"A point is fixed . . ."

A point is fixed at the
intersection between the
personal and the rest

of the cosmos, and that
nexus is the source
of the flood of speech

the desperate polyphony
of conflicting meanings
empties continually into,

all signs condensed into
a single line leading
out from this dust mote size

fraction of the history of
a very tiny star into the
silence everywhere around it

"In this river . . ."

In this river of stars and exile
longing rage apartness sorrow

love and hate light streams
through space tearing open a mouth

in its blank face giving its silence
a voice of joy and lamentation)

but as night comes on in dark
waves a black sun is rocked

and burning sand drifts across
agitated eyelids bereft of dream

slow solace for thought's
infinite twitching vigilance

Bathed

in the eerie phosphorous
green light that needles down
in the middle of the dream

she sleeps with mouth wide open
as if to gasp or cry out,
one hand raised up across her

forehead as if to ward off
a blow and the other one
clutching the covers which are

pulled up tight around her throat

Nodding

Drowsiness, identity drifting,
some kind of white

flower seen through isinglass,
stupor, bliss,

the moment before sleep
as the foretaste of the moment

before death—experience
of space receding, forgetfulness,

fate a self held mesh
in time like dust in a net

through which breath sifts with
the same kind of wet thin

cloth to skin feeling
as gauze or muslin

"Before dawn . . ."

Before dawn there you lie
sleepwalking circles in
your particularly nil
corner of eternity where

each routine circuit of
the mind plants another
iron pillar of thought around
which the next circuit's routed;

no change, no relief appears;
then, with a kick from ancient
energy of sun coming
up somewhere, sleep—sent to release

the hapless circuit traveler
from his pains—bears the
next instant into dream
fields of freedom; and life

happens to you all over again
in a way that, outside the moon cavern,
cannot be spoken of,
or thought, or named.

Sleepwalker's Way

The perpetuum mobile of my
Delusions is subject to drift,
Daydreams get in a sleepwalker's way
        nights on earth.

No one planned all this comical calamity,
Dislocated cosmography
Carte blanche for nitwits.
        Nights on earth

The subjectivity effect troubled
Othello also. He groaned his great
Hollow O over a world empty all
        nights on earth

Of the love of one lost girl.
That was not much to lose and yet a lot,
What he was left with was himself.
        Nights on earth

The head throbs. The heart goes haywire.
The subject identifies with the body
Of desire. Breath starts up again
        nights on earth.

Aubade

Truck gears grinding up Marin
Commuters descending pulse and
Fade into migraine forests
       to start the day

This sour music rises
Denatured lullaby
Mechanized and prefated
       to start the day

The head throbs and the slowly pounding heart
Fills body and mind with sorrow
Or joy according to chemical schema
       to start the day

Somnambulism

Echoed aria of threat opera
like mockingbird of pain forgotten

audible around every corner still
there is desire to explore the

ruined city of sidelong furtive
persons passing beneath the arching

blue ceiling the ancient dwarf
blackjack players in the diorama

whose walls are stripped away
everyone has a different fate and a

different desire the rhythmic tic of
the body of the orchestra conductor

an animated overture to
death bobbing up and down

Calling Infinity

A voice of resigned subsidence
As though in the same stroke
Everyone alive were speaking through you
Can't drive the fatalistic truth
Out of your anxious head

Each time the same old shadow falls across
The moment before sleep in
A life which will never be peaceful
Daylight fades but the shadow holds
No power over what's about to happen

On your roads of solitude, your streets of blood
Time narrows between two great
Vibrations of the sea: under the hood
Chromosome radio reports bad news with
A flash of pain from the voice of nature

Energy of the Pre-World as a Bungee Cable Jumper

Before the light radiates, where do you place it,
back there or out here in the pre-world
of street riot and armed detachments
grown commonplace, where the beam rotates like a mars light,
thought is as cautiously leashed as a bungee cable jumper

entrusted to a body beyond your body—is there
a body there, is it real, can you touch it
through the dark fire of the pre-world
that closes in? The presence of energy within
the elastic net fate weaves is the reckless

daredevil of the pre-world; fate allows it three
leaps, two snaps back, causing suffering,
causing hells; creating the body of desire,
suspending it in the vastness of space,
expanding it, disrupting it, offering it intense

resistance, whereof it can know itself.

The Pharoahs Sacrifice Themselves before Her

Time is the sweet cheat that unhinged
The Egyptians. The fugitive object
Of desire keeps fleeing, the symbol
Denoting speed in physics must now
Precede any expression of her value.
Algebra of desire yields to total
Calculus of need: instant nothingness
In which there flows an invisible current.
When it flows through the tomb, one is forced
To bow down and worship an obscure,
Mysterious and implacable goddess.

Time

2500 years Before Proust
Xerxes overthrew the stalwart
Lacedaemonians at Thermopylae.
He built a bridge of boats, allowed
His anima her autonomy and
His prow to be cut through by her armada,
Carving out a dark continent of desire
To identify with the object's body
That lasted 2500 years.
Through her nothingness there flowed
An invisible current. He sacrificed
Himself before her in an effort to
Recapture all the points of space she had
Ever occupied. It was vain—and when he took to
Thrashing the sea of events with rods
In an absurd attempt to punish
The engulfing of his treasure
Fate lost patience with his act,
His fleet was destroyed at Salamis
The same year he pillaged Athens.

Retro

Time is the sweet cheat that unhinged
Albertine's lover like the Pharoahs,

Flashback control studied in the pure
Cool silence of the memory bank

Where a train is parked before a dark
European forest in prehistoric

Half-light, shadows of the world dawn
Fading across the scene left to right.

With some archaic priest's prescient
Gesture destined to compress the durée

A mechanic bangs a hammer on a wheel,
The hollow ringing impact is deep-stored,

One day much later it will make a chord with
The light tapping impact of a spoon on a plate

In a heaven drained of all mood,
Reviving the fugitive body of desire

By involuntary illumination.
Every fraction of every fleeting instant there

Flash recall code keys that unlock and
Light up hidden chambers of lost worlds,

Stereopticon views of unpurchased universes,
Fate's rental properties furnished

With theatrical props and lights to
Compose an impossible perfect landscape.

The true air of paradise though is still the
Air of a paradise lost long ago.

Antiquarian

It is only mourning for the lost
Moment that has preserved like an echo of time
In these rustlings from the past
What the living moment continues to miss
The claim to happiness humans find denied
Them in this technified diorama world
They extract from albums of their idiosyncrasy
A hieroglyphic scrap of extinct emotion
Set adrift down pathways of forgotten life
As the human village prepares for its fate
The dream disintegrates but the shadow holds no power

Night Patrol

Out of Darkness I Came

The combination of blind drive and accident which make up what we call fate takes a different shape in the life of each one of us. My own profoundest intimations of the existence of anything outside myself were always muddled by a yearning for I knew not what and by the consciousness that something in the past had escaped me to which I could almost give a name. My confessions of a life given over to the emotions of the moment failing to satisfy my drive to expose my soul as it really was, I threw myself into the composition of a series of dialogues in which I split myself in several parts and allowed the most confidential and private truths of my personal history to be spoken of in their most secret light by the side of my nature which is the most demanding and least easily satisfied, and the most embarrassing wounds to be laid open by that side of my nature I hate the most, all so as to spare my true soul from slipping back into darkness without manifesting itself.

"Himself let him unknown contain"

Wyatt, with no insurance on his own head,
watching the execution of Anne Boleyn
from his cell in the Tower, while beyond
on Tower Hill her lovers also are executed,

reflects upon his wasted virtue and now
redundant innocence, rueful he ever did
let his name be known beyond the door of
his soul or hung his star from fate thrones.

"The enforced lapse . . ."

(Marguerite Yourcenar)

The enforced lapse into
despair of a writer
who does not write
having at last expired, in
midwinter of 1949,
shut up in a sleeper berth
on a westbound train
the French novelist,
resuming the
postponed obsession
of fifteen years,
takes up her life of
Hadrian in his own
voice—"a woman
does not recount her
own life, it is already
hard enough to give
some element of truth
to the utterances
of a man"—working
late into the night
on the Twentieth
Century Limited
between New York and
Chicago, all through the
next day in the
station restaurant

in Chicago, waiting
out a snowstorm when
her train's delayed, and
then again writing till dawn
alone in the observation
car of the Super Chief
arrowing across the
transparent night
hemmed in by black spurs
of the American Cordillera
and by the eternal
pattern of the stars

By the time she reaches
Taos she has written
in a single great rush
the passages on food
love sleep and the
knowledge of men
and begun to transport herself
into another's body and soul

A year later, in a night
of freezing cold and almost
polar silence on Mount
Desert Island, off the
Maine coast, she writes of
the weight of
sickbed sheets on the body
in the smothering heat
of a July day in Baiae
in the year 138, and of
the almost inaudible sound
of the ocean, which becomes
the last image in the
mind of the dying emperor

"I tried to go as far
as the last sip of
water, the last
spasm of pain"

In the end
from the original version
of 1934 she keeps
only one sentence
the one which first
established her point
of view
the one in which
she had first found
the window into
another mind, permitting her
to live in a past time:
"I begin to discern
the profile of my death."

Spiritual

(Eric Dolphy with John Coltrane
at Village Vanguard, 1961)

Men have these kinds
of gleams in their skulls
which however briefly
deny the influence of
the fate which is written
for them in another kind
of book, one bound
and complete before
birth or history. Going
through life a man
performs specific
acts at specific
times, and some of
these become creations
which remain alongside
other creations in the
minds of those who
survive. And then they
too die, and fate
defines everything.

Fate

The earliest words for it are transparent
Metaphors, *moira, aisa*
Denoting share or portion, those distinctive
Events of a person's life which carry
Change like the scar of a laser
A talisman stamped into the
Genetic chain by god, it is
A flash of the hand of nature,
Divine anger defining energy
Destiny of all men being death
As Achilles lashed out at Thetis
I don't argue with this any more
Than a bell with its flaw, the
Crack of determination
Under the hood of the chromosome
Diminished thirds, the car radio
The flow of words is control
Orphée, the words hang in the air
Only a poem of time if you know it
(This before religion or logic)

Moira

You must not change your life plan over
Divine airspace reserved for
Vector traffic of the ion
Charged hyper soul swarm

Through that void outer zone of cloud nebulae
Where the star frequencies (her messages)
Get lost in silence and a soft
Blue dust left by the memory of light

Moira's Messages

Chance, an external compulsion
Abrupt as a U-turn
Is planted in the stars
By her spinning fingers

No parking for faith
In cloud nebulae where
The roads of deep space
Are paved with silence

And a soft blue dust
Left by the memory of light
Which creates line noise
On the transmission frequency

Over which she sends
Out all life messages
When she pulses the system
The chance options multiply

The Moirai

In the burlesque fantasy of Seneca
They produce from a little box
The spindles of Claudius and his
Similarly ill-fated cronies.

Tapes of their greatest hits.
The ancients laughed themselves to death.
Earlier, weird tales
Tell of strange, difficult women

Living on tv dinners in some
Bat cave in the Arcadian Ozarks.
We see them fiddling in the mist
With armfuls of tapes and spools.

These twisted, twisting
Sisters—gene-splicing
The species into the ground,
Word-processing the future

Into concrete—these twisted,
Twisting sisters, doing death's work
In the bullshit of the myth—
Being right is their only excuse.

Fate Spinners in Time-Editing Studio, Eternity Blvd., 2 A.M.

Hesiod attributes those Bette Davis peepers of the Moirai—
Bulging with perpetual adrenal reaction
At the sheer brink of a revulsion
As precipitous as a fjord—

To a massive thyroid malfunction,
An overdose of glandular distaste
Produced by all the accumulated dismalness
These doomy sisters have had to lay eyes on.

Baby Book Fate Dream

Inadequate illumination
In the Museum of Tomb Paintings
Sarcophagus like big xerox machine
Everything vaguely Egyptian
Book of the Dead-ish

Three hooded figures
Two women and a taller
Bearded man in between
I keep running into them
In my copy shop of the soul dream

They sing together gravely chanting
The song is copied on tape
And mechanically transcribed
In the baby book of my fate
Which I get kept from reading.

The Domestic Life of Ghosts

Whoso list to haunt could do worse than to
Obtain the license, get the picture.
Spook finders must find spooks to put the face,
Name and space coordinates together.
What is kept in the mind perimeter
Retains a wild autonomy through fate.

I will retreat to the precorporate.
Let fate have what is fate's and allow
This spirit to slip through time's difficult
Nets with the devious fingers of
A wild wind, while I run along behind.

Moodsville

Red Garland interpreting Bird's "Constellation"
You will hear a lot of noises racing
                        through subterranean chambers
But all are constant with the sound laconic
You must not let yourself be run by your voice

The definition of articulate
Tempo arithmetic like lights clinking in glass cubes
To create quiet trick semaphores

A Garland of Red

There is an ancient myth behind every place
Red drops his hands on the keyboard in despair
And they fall exactly into place
An instant locking like aphrodite and god
Wrapped up in each other by the gulf
Where pineal moonlight in the mode of feeling
Pours in on the color module shore
                  north of corpus christi

Rojo

While Red set sail on a junkboat
Brown took a chinese lotus
A star called its child Altair to create White
And Red followed Miles farther south of the border
To a rapid orbit of what is in your mind

Slowly as the color module continues to spin
A window of opportunity to the fourth world
Opens inward for red shift engravers
To plant on blue terraria of the night sky
A six-eight figure of eternity

Or

(for Dexter Gordon)

the disjunctive conjunction, severing
in space what in human time
it connects as the mood moves farther
in, and farther up—with feeling
that everything might be everything
as Dexter lopes across green stars to catch
and pass Wardell Gray in blue space on *The Chase*

Motion, 1953

Rita Hayworth & Stan Getz
dancing in a west coast
airplane shack
made of light wood

everything looks
aerodynamic
or like laminated
in the painted hangar

takeoff into a light wind
moving through
a baffle of bamboo
deck rolling slightly—

in ancient myth
every place is sacred
swaying bodies come apart
tropic clouds race

a paper moon
the jungle more safe
than the beach
in a cool tsunami

Coral

The hole time burns in my breathing
The gardenia of your mouth and skin on green
Dolphin street gypsy cabs drive through stars,
Fates double park to
Pass time taking you in,
Fathom the impulses of your inner life
Some fragile coral
           green undersea thing
Haunted by your eroticism
Which is like that of cats or
                 birds of prey

Theatre

Hunting and gathering in sexual refuge theatre
While fireflies escape summer night dark props
Unfolding fruity pink inside mysterious wire
Strung by ghost riders across a chilled out sky
Painted on the stars' hard phosphorus glaze

Though the actors intermingle with crushing heat
An arrow of song still flies toward the wings alone
Lassoing the delirious complexities of this plot
Into the shape of a tale short and easy
Seen through the mist sleeve that encloses Sirius

Mist Sleeve Flight

Solemn light in morning drizzle early
Concept of space breathing in the music
Wisps of pale color drip from trees
Love sleeping in the other room
In walks Krishna's sister with eyes
Of wanderer on prehistoric planet
Gentle and beautiful in the music
As colors of dream mist drain away
It's only a paper moon sex thing
Occurring several thousand years ago
Which you've again forgotten to remember now

On Marine Silence Street

Hurry up my lute wake and strum your tune
Before this lump of atoms is no longer me
No lost time in the diorama of eternity
Nothing can stop the rising of human sap
Across endless billboards of blank aqua
Low muted notes of unseen pocket trumpets
Draw sulky arcs through your sunlit bugle glare
Off there in dark young autonomy shining
In your feminine presence I've always felt weak
When love inflicts its infinite papercuts
Over the black starlight's dim *éclat*
I don't know how ordinary guys keep going

My Hypertrophic Devotion

meaning by possession total possession
subject and object identifying
à la the siamese model so that
if someone got in the way of
the roentgen rays of my exaggerated

jealousy concerning your person
that someone would in all likelihood be you
in the form of the angel guardian of your
autonomy which fills all space
with the impenetrability of your temporal moment

Personal Angel Glimpsed

In my own time I watch the light of nature falling
Through the trees shift and move across her skin.
I know it is the light of glory at play in the fields of quanta
Imparting to the personal an immaterial skin-shine,
The fine aura of a phosphorescent life-seltzer
Which continually sifts and moves through the temporal.

According to the Book of Changes it is this which
Fate offers me as a rain check for eternity,
Time on my side to reflect the light of her personal
Glory falling on air and becoming solid,
While the fluidity of infinity drinks
My mind leaving me eternally retarded.

Ace of Destiny

Quite outside and beyond the personal
Ah soldier girl I'm lost in your chlorine eyes
Let us whirl one enormous second in paradise
Where fire that must flame is with apt fuel fed

Pony up time I'm slammed to the planet
On the other end of the line I hear your starlike
Autonomy shining beyond mortality's
Wild nightingale trill of sudden judgment

Egypt, Everything

Egypt, everything moves across paper stars in abstract night skies, wadis, arroyos, wild old Arab Arizonas, playas of abrupt moons, mesas over which hang in a great arc an ivory crescent sky goddess who spans with her body the whole inverted bowl of intensely dark Navajo inking.

Culebra Cascabel

Before infinity drinks the sun, Sleepwalker rambles in the desert. Circe of Egypt has dispatched him on these terrible patrols, while this cold shoreline moon waxes and dwindles and is replaced by a new ocean pulling the sun toward the poison sac of her green eyes.

Autorotation without Gravity

On the gulf in an airplane shack made of light everything looks aerodynamic like laminated parts of the body if you have sleepwalked all night following star maps stitched together out of fabulous cloth spun from a single silver thread of quiet thought.

Night Patrol

Night, clouds, I know where you are going. Sleepwalker's fate's to dream with eyes wide open. Everything that happens now was ancient news long ago: your body glides through it with eyes wide open. Law rules everything, but mercy forms a great arc over everything, and everything disappears through forgetting—forgetting, and being forgotten.

Human Life

Withdrawal

When the gods who once ruled over the
doings of this earth withdrew to
move on to a new star in the far
out dust of eternity, giving us
up for lost, leaving us to our
suicidal drives, their going away
present was the indeterminacy
that gives us the power to write our
own fate scripts once more, as we die out.

A Theory of the Universe

Nature is out there as
Well as in here to access
From worlds burning at the
Outer visible edges of these

Planets like black emotions
Looming on your display screen
The exploding universe throws
Its optical mouse at you

And the pull of the moon makes
You believe in the program
As the antelope believes in the raging
Ideology of the lion

Narcissism

Kneeling like the White Rock Girl
over the cool pool of its special
yearnings to be nurtured and healed,
to have its soul soothed in the common
uniqueness of its wound,
the language of Codependency and
Inner Children murmurs of a civilization
which has made its own mirror
image its most interesting story.

Human Life

Always behind my back I hear
The spastic clicking of jerked knees
And other automatic reactions
Tracking me through the years to where
Time's winged chariot is double
Parked near the eternity frontier
And in such moments I want to participate
In human life less and less
But when I do the obligatory double take
And glance behind me into the dark green future
All I see stretching out are vast
Arizona republics of more

West of Eden

Wincing in a Lost Angeles future glare
I gasp agape amid think tanks,
Fleeing the harsh light of an agenda.

Forthwith time rebates human affinity
Removing the dark horror of things
From my tongue with sighs, and touching

Of strings with toughened fingers.
Overhead the rising moon looms
This selfsame revenant gravity notwithstanding.

October

Fall—dust of
decaying

leaves in air as
haze of all

things decomposing
settling

earthward—
"I's" blurred

view & memorial
sinking back into

subjective sludge
of old age

"Walked into state . . ."

Walked into state
office building
in flat white
light of cold
overcast that,
without sun,
makes all days
seem alike—
boat adrift on
ocean sans shore
floats aimless
on endless waves
falling and
again lifting

Ancestors

1946   suddenly
to remember how it
was to walk into the
kitchen of one's now
dead ancestors and see the
brown gold or porous
sepia light falling
ground reels under
that sudden feeling
of how the world will
feel in this place long
time from now, when
remembered by no one

1968

All the while I was
being numbered and
stored by history
as an example
of something
as flat and thin
as a picture
in a textbook
or an image
on film
I remained under
the illusion I was
merely living

Terminator Too

Poetry, Wordsworth
wrote, will have no
easy time of it when
the discriminating

powers of the mind
are so blunted that
all voluntary
exertion dies, and

the general
public is reduced
to a state of near
savage torpor, morose,

stuporous, with
no attention span
whatsoever; nor will
the tranquil rustling

of the lyric, drowned out
by the heavy, dull
coagulation
of persons in cities,

where a uniformity
of occupations breeds

cravings for sensation
which hourly visual

communication of
instant intelligence
gratifies like crazy,
likely survive this age.

Sounding Chinese at Inspiration Point

Nice spring day off big white cloud
At Inspiration Point escaping time wars
Poet takes book & wine bottle up into Mist Mountains

Since only available agenda is rhyming with silence
Seeking window of opportunity on a wall
I disguise what I have to say by sounding Chinese

Such as stars are now darker and farther away
They take deeper drinks because space is
Drying out afraid to think own thoughts

Administered citizen achieving condition of robot
In public mind things not so good these days
Nor in wrong run will it matter to Tu Fu

Day Detail—Low Light of Afternoon

Pleasant northeast wind, 2 monarch
butterflies being idly blown
through the ivy—airplane sounds,
traffic sounds, sounds of someone
hammering. Being, idly blown
from star to star on a spore
makes it across all that nothing
just to have a home, like the boll
weevil in the Leadbelly song,
belly to belly and bone to bone
just to keep from lying down
alone in cold eternity soul hangar

The Silence of the Lambs

Cold opal eyes gleaming
with the half-masked
predatory acuity of a
hunting bullet hawk's,
Robinson Jeffers lurks
with a sleepwalker lean
outside the Oaks moviehouse
in my Solano Avenue
fate dream. The people
waiting in line to see Silence
of the Lambs don't notice even
when like some manic and elated
Ezekiel of the church
of the latter day desperation
saints he rolls those old
hollow eyes back up into the
unburied hatchet of his
elongated acromegaloid
cranium and begins intoning
in a cracked vatic moan:
Consider, O
little man, the earthward
directed stare of the vacant
minded domestic sheep
which has lost all alertness
in its centuries of depending
on someone else to do

its looking and thinking for it:
it has leased out to hominids
the responsibilities of its senses
as have the hominids in turn
to their incredible machines;
consider on the other hand
a mountain deer tracked
by a big cat, daintily
testing every breeze, alert to
spring at the least crackle of
a twig and flee with great
arching bounds, repeating
in every twitch and stride
the precision gloryings
of the creation experiment;
but these sheep—his cold
baleful eyes come open again
and he scrutinizes the Saturday
night cinema crowd with a
righteous preacher's bearing—
a concrete pasturage will
be their pathetic eternal
burying ground. A black
and white squad car cruises
up Solano; the dead poet ambles
off at an odd angle down
the avenue, his raving
eliding into demented
cackling laughter that wafts
off over the heads of the
unconcerned moviegoers.

In the Dark Mountains, Brilliant

Seeing death bobbled by destiny, touched
By descent of life's blinking eyelid
From clear sky sooner than hope advertised
Nature says be cool, nothing ever mattered
More than spending a smooth eternity
Watching this punk purple martin splash
In a trout pool of the Sierra Nevada

Before dying, being released from time
And becoming the feather glance light
Surrendered in these deep blue wing vibrations
Flashing against the grayish matte air
To establish a phrase intelligible
In no other tongue than those that rustle through
The lower ponderosa and blue oak forests

Fireflies

Out of a blow dryer Santa Ana rolling
firefly showers down scrub oak
and eucalyptus canyons in wild
cascades explodes a bloody charcoal

cloud, and ghost smoke closes
in on trees that feel gun crazy
nervous in coverts of the night
as Oakland burns down toward the bay.

Later quieting evening beams up a cold
opalescent moon above fogged ruins,
flickering gas mains are what remains
to glimmer in the charged glowworm dark.

After the Fire—The Woman

in pathos, seemingly numb,
picking through a vagueness
of ashes for pieces of the
past. *Home* a memory catalog
of desire and need and
refuge in the mind but,
in her hand, only a smoke
darkened pink ceramic duck
as fossil testament of it.

"First cold winter twilights . . ."

First cold winter twilights despite this
week's richmond refinery fire
never more perfect even the
burned and corrupt air stunning
saffron violet orange indigo
becoming blood red as sun descends
with a delayed shudder or retarded
tremor into ocean fire
and night begins to close in
over the whole sky from other
(eastern) end—a deep blue bowl

or dish inverted convex
glass dome extruded
pyrex lid over boundless
now starless ozone
depleted spaces of what
must become known as end
times—last hundred years of
human habitation rendering
in view of coming loss the
earth in ever more damaged form even
more beautiful than ever before

De Ira Dei

Anger is a necessary element in the character of God
given what is to be looked upon
in the mirror of an extinguished creation
with an eye that shines through the hole
in the ozone, clouded by frozen tears

Trout Kill on the Sacramento

Pathfinding in dark byways
and searching pools, shooting deeper
channels of another world's
pitches and reaches; mute blue

spaces, intuitions of the
sightless, soundings of light in cool
alleys of current; aerated
displacement of water around

smooth propulsion that loses
resistance as it moves into
a greenish ooze of lethal
effluvium from another world.

Milky Turquoise Cloud

Milky turquoise cloud
makes river quiet
wherever it goes.
This is power. This

is the destroyer
of worlds unloosed
from a tank car. This
is human error,

which says, Well, OK,
so we make mistakes,
but without us, who's
going to run things?

"In the bond scandals . . ."

In the bond scandals,
having stumbled into

a free market wonder
land in which value

has come to seem forever
detached from even the

thought of actual labor,
there grows among the young

men on The Street
an assumption that

they can do anything,
a confidence bubble,

a prodigious enlargement,
like the engorgement of an

overstimulated gland, of
the horizon of economic

possibility—as if
the impossible were suddenly

possible, and the soul uplifted

Sleepwalker

Sleepwalker is henry hill, the wiseguy who survives
in witnessprotectionville, somewhere in the sun belt
Sleepwalker never exactly dies, he is the mercenary
workman spared by the driven

killers of history—achilles drunk on adrenalin and
endorphins, lurching from the tent to avenge
patroclus, roland, hannibal at cannae,
lee at fredericksburg by

the river of infinity, the dust full of gods
and a fine aerosol spray of blood
and tissue—*ergon* is homer's word
for what men do in battle, a unit of work

to undo so many, yet the work is never complete
even in death's strong house
there is always something left to dream,
a ghost breath, a phantom

Sleepwalker's Fate

Sleepwalker, though you toted your dead comrade's M-60
Over the Ia Drang, across Death Valley
Through Bong Son and up Hill 875
With the vindictive-aggressive mania of an Achilles

And poured hot steel across paddy into treeline
Until the metal bolt melted down to a glowing
Red like dawn over Cambodia in your hands
Your courage won't get your tape off the spindle

When the Sisters throw down on you with the heavy
Firepower only an editor of your fate can produce
You will end up on the cutting room floor
For all your phallocentric adrenalin

Nobody will care how many barrels
You burned up getting to be a spook

The Door Gunner to the Moment
(A Shau Valley 1968)

It's a sleepwalker's fate to dream with his eyes
wide open. His dance with the moment allows him
to know what he is doing at the same time he does not
know what is going on. Knowing he can't ever watch
out well enough to save himself he must always knock
himself out to watch out every fleeting moment.
The jungle canopy from above is a seafloor of heaven, covering
and concealing everything. Agitation of the rotor
blades gives way to weird calm and everything
grows still. You forget everything, you remember
everything, you know what you know. A green reef of hill
erupts with muzzle flashes and thin puffs of white
smoke. You know everything has laws but mercy
forms a great arc over everything, suspending laws
of cause and effect in a great forgetting determined
long ago. The rush of thin air into your face
is fate. The world rocks and the rotation of the
blades is suddenly disrupted. Reality starts
to spin yet still events lurch forward with
a circular sameness, you are blown back against the struts,
everything that happens now was ancient news long ago,
a zombie glides through it in your body with your eyes wide
open.

Eternity

The god of war assured King Arsounas, "Do not be fooled by words. No life is taken. Know that no one was ever born, nor does anyone die." In the violent mini-eternity of the warrior, combat is conducted according to a ritual formal as song: no one is ever born, no one can ever die. The left-handed rockabilly guitarist whose left arm was severed by an RPG round at Dak To has come back to life in a part of my body that died long before we started to patrol this part of the river of eternal woe. His life is mine though I never lived it. The violent backwash of the rotors is crimsoned by a fine aerosol spray of blood while a loudspeaker amplifies the goddess' excited laughter.

The Commanders

When the Medina Luminous Division marched into
Divine Anger in the Energy Refuge Theatre—
Bottle green starlight chaos,
The river of infinity, the dust full of gods—
The Commanders felt good about themselves,
They said, Say hello to Allah
And the Medina Luminous Division said hello to God.

Next the In God We Trust Division was drawn out of K City,
It was Bravo-20 on the Basra Road,
Rockeye and Hellfire lived up to the instruction manuals.
As the fireballs digested the convoys of helpless
The Commanders paused to gas up
Their FA-18s, their hummvees, their Apaches
Then moved out to incinerate the Hammurabi.

Public life is not so great these days.
The Private Life of the Master Race,
The allegory hidden inside The Commanders,
Hints the fault lies not in the stars but in the cell.
No one has time to tell tales to idiots.
Nation of nothing but idiot fatality,
Agenda rhyming with silence rubbing off.

40 Days

sleepwalker can never die
he is the chemical soldier
composite of latex
and atropine,
hellfire, warthogs,
desolation, pride,
apaches, lasers,
dust

devils swirling,
screaming fire
deaths, machine
worship, young blond
pilots flashing thumbs
up, excited smiles
of interviewed
military wives, shrapnel-

paced rockeye
anti-personnel
bombs spraying
death like fireflies
over a texas barbecue
of human flesh
stretching sixty miles
across open desert,

armageddon
over eden, algebraic
mosaic
of witchcraft, dot
pattern magic of omens
and signs,
victims never
knowing what

hit them, vivid
delivery of hell
to nineveh,
incendiary
reduction of tissue
to shadows on the sand,
incineration of boots
with human feet still

in them, pain,
mania,
technology,
history, delirious
victims bleeding,
eagle with the brains
of a weak and

frightened victim in
its beak, unhappy
fate, grief,
shame, helpless
rage

Desert Wars

World speeding toward
Bottle green starlight chaos
Nintendo fuse of blood
To destroy Sumerian language
In a video glass ambulance

Ash and tetrahedra

Large twisted blocks
Across the blue black plain
Pencils of wheeling light
Red sandstone skies

Minarets of volcanic glass
Soft black sand weaves
Gangster fez of dawn
Orange gold ignition on black
Telephone pole cigarets
Whole sky lights up & hums
Then huge roar comes

Daring to Be the Same

Without spectators there is no spectacle. After the last of the televised war programming, viewers report a vacancy in their lives. People ache to do the right thing, a survey shows, but they are confused and usually end up doing exactly the opposite. No one knows why, but inflicting pain upon officially designated victims seems optimally fulfilling. We verbalize for the Question Man our need to "feel good about ourselves," a deep hunger like that of irresolute souls who roam the higher realms of the underworld in a continual restless anxiety, and once more smoke rises from the stages of rock concerts as at Roman sacrifices.

Heralding the pop goddess' coming with dutiful pomp and circumstance like regimental janissaries of some sulking imperial potentate, a cordon of jogging Gallic policemen in full dress regalia precedes her white limousine as it cruises to a showy halt before the palace.

Out she steps, magnetic in a rose-colored kimono. From the throng of spellbound onlookers, who have never dared imagine her as anything but a platinum blond, her heavy brown curls elicit stunned gasps. At a safe distance behind police restraining barriers they feast on her as deliriously as famished refugees ravaging a relief truck.

Moving slowly up the palace staircase she pauses every few steps to bask in her fame and pose for photos. Like glowing fruit in the emir's hanging gardens, or detonated grenades, flash explosions fill the soft night air.

She ascends the stairs, a charged filament, rose-colored sexual electricity conducted through space as if by remote control in a world that is an enormous studio, while the ambient

106

pseudo-orchestral din of pulsing polyrhythmic synthesizer music reaches a shuddering climax—a thousand jackboots stomping at once against the back-beat, demented shrieking of a violated toy doll overdubbed. A hallucinated yet oddly predictable lyric pounds into a billion brains, while video of her sucking on a coke bottle pours down two billion eyeballs. Model yachts glide across the glassy surface of the satellite reflecting pools around the outdoor fountain at Eden Roc. It is a society of a trillion fantasies daring to be the same.

At the top of the steps she lets the kimono slip from her shoulders, there are squeals and screams of delight as the blue and red spotlights nibble at her underwear, which is exotic virginal white. The breast cups of her bra, modeled to simulate warheads of guided missiles, project out with an attitude of uplift and thrust into a target-rich consumer environment, computer-driven to the mark, and the screaming never stops.

Diary of Desert War

(1990–1991)

SUNDOWN, NASTY COUNTRY— over a stony plain in armored cars, like dogs nosing a rhinoceros

ARMORED DESERT-WATCHING— morning, driving over smooth sand
and flint—low pale sun behind us

LITTLE SHELTERS, BRANCHES and palm-leaves, deep moon, breathing the light—a cigarette as reward

GLIDING ACROSS SHINING flat desert two nights and four days with the wadi wells to help us find our way—coming up the plateau fast, roaring exhausts

CAMEL COUNTRY—BLACK flints, marly limestone, wells and ruins, hill villages, gazelle desert, rice-night, coffee-fire, cool upland stars crying

TALK IN TENT of unknown stars, suns beyond suns, distance unseen, stars behind world's end, turned on greater worlds—at dawn, down a bank of chalk—flint-capped hollow white conical hills shone as snow in sunshine

SCOURED DAZZLING PLAIN of grey packed sand colors, porphyry, green basalt, pure white stratum carpet, particles caught like diamonds, hard glassy waves miles in front of us

IN DARKNESS, BANDS of air stirring, neutral heavy moon down dead, hot black air-narrows, lonely desert, immense shadow-dark doors above our heads, refracted shafts of sky across the great valley

OVER SUGAR-LIKE damp sawdust for miles up valley with knolls of green stone and green shadows so blended they gave a sense of straight lines

FLOODS OF WHITE, flat reach of earth, hum of flies hovering over veiled sleep

DELTA WADI BROODING, twenty miles away the great hills
dancing, heat feathery, night of swelling sand and coffee

GREAT DELTA DARK in flood, dried beds twisting across—beyond,
the invisible sea, Tigris a mile wide with lines of sand and clay
divided, mud flaking, dead air—the river bed laced, tangled, dusty
as old bone

REACHED THE FAR bank, ground suddenly cleared, deep brown flood water went further north through a huge plain of sand—soldiers splashing in the water—mist rose out of the cold black night—moonless stars over white seas of fog, luminous world moving through life without warning

GUARD POSITION, EVENING, yellow foil declining down the angle of ridges, rays and planes, flints reflecting black diamond flame sky

MENTAL TIME AT nightfall—guns over our plateau

FLAT MILKY STARLIGHT and cool air—desert full of sounds, scents, grass ebbed and flowed, dying stars shifting compass somewhere in deep calculating, a gasp on the horizon blacker than sky

TEN MILES ACROSS one huge mud-flat—armored cars wheeled into
sunset cliffs red against the sky

EAST SLOWLY, INTO a distance-blue hazy plain—long shadows, morning river of sunlight poured on every stone—northward, a little later, over low sandstone slabs ranged up to map the great strung bow of desolation

WHITE MILKY NIGHT, filling up time—sleeping moon, distant noises, a darker mesh star-fever—before us a great dark lava range and black sandstone cliffs—air-suspended stillness of the valleys

PLUNGED INTO A lava-field drowned in sand too soft to be called sand—wind very still across valley—up the further slopes, settled, spread the carpet, sat while coffee was made hot before dawn

BAKED—WE STARTED across lava waves with a covering of cinder—water-systems scoring yellow lines across blue-black land for miles, features colored like a map—noon till three, uneasy, scorched road mounted spines of disordered causeways—sand-laden ground, orange-rind sunlight, faded blue-grey basalt tetrahedra rubbed and rounded like tesserae

LAVA TRACK THROUGH black ash—beyond, another lava-field, older—flat rank desert, unfortunate place

INLAID BLUE ROADS across clean yellow mud ridges, bars of blue-grey stone, a stretch of jet-black mud, and afterwards soft, black sandstone rising from blackness—waves of wind-blown decay, ominous passing of time through hour after hour of twisted cooling lava and scrub wadi

TWISTED DREAMS—NAKED dark eternity, lava gone iron-blue, twisted crusts of rock lava skull, crystallized fronds of metallic rock, broken river of lava—broken bones

HOT SLEEP, FLIES, yellow tent-hole sunlight, ringing of coffee, distant shots, drum of blood deeper

RODE INTO BROWN hills—death in the air

ASSAULT BEFORE DAWN— bombs splashed two thousand yards of stones across the plain—later, men rising like the day of judgment, to nothing

ORDERED BACK WESTWARDS over the broad basin of imperceptible evil, down ashy slopes into the horrible water pools and open wells—sunset, some stroke of flame cut open the immense mud-flat for miles to southward—eastward, the marshes mirage-blurs of steely blue

EMPTY MIRAGE SPACES, heat waves and sunlight crystal clear—wild birds, alarmed by our exhausts, in flight past the lava fields—hard swamp, blue walls, silent silken palms—stillness, fear, throbbing of grazing airplanes

HUNDRED MILES TO new base—electrum shield reflecting sunlight, faster pace out to open flint desert, glowing metal, broiling drivers, blistering day, each soldier apart in heat and sweat—dusty, oily, naked shapes, they hardly spoke, inhuman in their lives

AFTERNOON, ARMORED TOO heavy—sank in, heavy going, heated up—bursts, stoppings, hot levering and pumping, thin tempers, sulky drivers swinging long curves over shallow valleys, haze distance white-lit by pouring sun—late afternoon, roared at forty miles an hour across wells alive with fires—pitching camp, war rations—drivers of supply column half-mutinous, complaining

EVENING FIRE OUT over the ridge, coming off the slopes beyond—black silent reek of smoke, ferment of soil in the steely desert wind, cloistered air, fifty miles blank country

AIRPLANE WENT DOWN out over the plains, like chance-winnowed corn

BURNING RUMORS IN the new moon—pushed cautiously into hunting-places, night journeys, units lost touch

MIDNIGHT MOON WHITENESS frozen and shadowless—night birds flying in wheeling circles—after, night empty again, we slept in wormwood—tired laughter, airplanes had not found us

NERVOUS, WE MOVE at night—the road a death-trap

TWO AIRPLANES SEARCHING the sky—third ranged nearer, fired, burned and turned—return spiteful, clever bombs swooped low, one each time—we crept among stones, bombs tore over—we lay open to attack in the shadow of the desert

OPEN DESERT BOMBING—defenseless under repeated attack, troops red-eyed, trembling, left useless by fear, dangerous to themselves

AIR FIGHTING UNFOLDING, quick flies moving the wind while our people lay like lizards among stones waiting for the next bomb—restless dusty sunlight splashed over

DEMOLITION NIGHT FANTASTIC—fire fell for three hours in a maze of light—we turned back, running northward out of flame, flashes and explosions—southward, a green shower of tracer across the dark—above, howling terror of luminous attack

SUNLIGHT AND FLIES, noise, dust, smoke, wild energy, killing, the fire-box torn open

SUNSET—RED WINGS fiery across the great pit-floor of damp sand

A MEMORY BEFORE paradise—dark stars unable to cast light, echoes of torn black moonlight—tongue from some unknown speech

SLEEPLESS NIGHT—PUSHED forward and reached the company hospital at dawn, heard the war news . . .

Dark Continent
(1965–1986)

The Lake

Lake Life, I want to take a bath
In you and forget death
Waits at the muddy bottom
Although I live in the tree
Of poetry and sing, I have no
Water wings
And fear death by drowning

Sometimes I get a pain in my breath
Apparatus, then I stop breathing
Long enough to count the trees
Across the lake, and the leaves
Whirling on the water
Start to sink slowly, in circles
That down deep, become straight lines

I'm on an Island

Do not try to adopt me
I am not a pigmy soothed
Boy or baby hitchhiker saint

What is wrong suddenly
Is that I swallow a cold
Blast of air, I mean fright

Spill coffee on my book
And hear the kinks
In the great universe

The warp in the coffin
Phantom men fly out of
Anywhere in this world

Easter Sunday

Someone has frozen the many-storeyed houses
Under this planetarium
A brilliant silence like a foghorn

A perfect frieze before the complications
Arrive with dialogue and
The olives of daily life

This brown Barcelona paper
Thrown onto the blue stone of the day
Makes everyone stop leaving

Through the light in a glass of wine you see them
Under the hot sky of the glacier
Placing their bets then boarding the funeral train

Dark Continent

The journey in darkness has a trivial jargon
For the cans of black coffee and ears like sprigs
Of an intelligent listening flower

This agitation is a kind of heavy wood
That you could hold a candle to
And never alter its unendurableness

There is nothing to do about voyaging
Fears except to jerk their brilliance
Out ahead of you like a rushlight like this

But what is illumined in the jungle large
Is a girl in narrow white sashes
Seated in your room at your writing desk

Momentum

I saw the busy street you crossed the last time I saw you
as the river of time, carrying you away forever.
Your pale coat was swirling like a leaf in the current
in the crowd of anonymous bodies hurrying back to work.

I turned around and started to walk in the other direction
but because of the tears in my eyes I failed to see a dentist
standing outside the entrance to his office and collided with
     him,
knocking him down.

Change

Stepping down was like being born
out of the flank
of a bus, like Dionysus from
Zeus. The guts of the pavement
lay open under flags and gazers.

As we passed the bank and needle,
still on the bus, you gazed
out and then it seemed I was Dionysus
and you Diana or another in the bays.
I rushed toward you as if Zeus
heard you when you turned to me, amazed,
and said "It's strange to see the world through
your arm."

Afternoons

It's fine to wake up and hug your knees
my knees
when I have run out of fire fluid
I rush back to bed

the feeling of paws on my knees
petals and wings
little hair,
why have you gone

I sing that in my head
being alone is a song
a cigarette in bed
it's better not to touch the ceiling
but if love attaches a band-aid
from the ceiling to your head
there's nothing to do but recognize it.

Superballs

You approach me carrying a book
The instructions you read carry me back beyond birth
To childhood and a courtyard bouncing a ball
The town is silent there is only one recreation
It's throwing the ball against the wall and waiting
To see if it returns
One day
The wall reverses
The ball bounces the other way
Across this barrier into the future
Where it begets occupations names
This is known as the human heart a muscle
A woman adopts it it enters her chest
She falls from a train
The woman rebounds 500 miles back to her childhood
The heart falls from her clothing you retrieve it
Turn it over in your hand the trademark
Gives the name of a noted maker of balls

Elastic flexible yes but this is awful
You say
Her body is limp not plastic
Your heart is missing from it
You replace your heart in your breast and go on your way

You (V) (after Hölderlin)

O Earth Mother, who consents to everything, who forgives
    everything
don't hide like this   and tell

Her Power is sweetened in these rays, the Earth before her
        conceals the children
of her breast in her cloak, meanwhile we feel her,

and the days to come announce
that much time has passed and often one has felt
        a heart grow for you inside his chest
They have guessed, the Ancients, the old and pious Patriarchs,
        and in secret they are, without even knowing it,
        blessed
in the twisted chamber, for you, the silent men
but still more, the hearts, and those you have named Amor,
or have given obscure names, Earth, for one is shamed
to name his inmost heart, and from the start however man
when he finds greatness in himself and if the Most High
    permits,
he names it, this which belongs to him, and by its proper name
and you are it, and it seems
                    to me I hear the father say
to you honor is granted from now on
and you must receive songs in its name,
and you must, while he is distant and Old Eternity
        becomes more and more hidden every day,
take his place in front of mortals, and since you will bear
        and raise children for him, his wish

is to send anew and directly toward you men's lives
when you recognize him   but this
directive which he inscribes in me is the rose
Pure sister, where will I get hold, when it is winter, of these
flowers, so as to weave the inhabitants of heaven crowns
                    It will be
as if the spirit of life passed out of me,
because for the heavenly gods these signs
of love are flowers in a desert   I search for them, you are
          hidden

"Like musical instruments . . ."

Like musical instruments
Abandoned in a field
The parts of your feelings

Are starting to know a quiet
The pure conversion of your
Life into art seems destined

Never to occur
You don't mind
You feel spiritual and alert

As the air must feel
Turning into sky aloft and blue
You feel like

You'll never feel like touching anything or anyone
Again
And then you do

Love (after La Rochefoucauld)

Like ghosts,
   much talked about,
      seldom seen.

The Last Poem (after Robert Desnos)

I've dreamed so much of you
Walked so much
Talked so much made love to your shadow
So much that there's nothing left of you
What is left
Of me is a shadow
Among shadows but 100
Times more shadowy than the rest
A shadow that will come
To rest
In your life in which the sun
Is so much.

I Was Born to Speak Your Name

I knew the tune
It was my song
Even before you came along
Yet only then did I perceive its meaning

This *you* I wished for
This desired Other of whom
I spoke so glowingly in poems
I never knew its name

When I lifted its arms up
I noticed tiny wings
That's all I knew
The rest was Muselike
Anonymous this "you"

So I guess those poems
Were like phonecalls to the future
I think I had your number
Knew what I was looking for
Even before I found it
In the face directory

And luckiest of all
Your human substance
Was life's loveliest
Far as I could see

As if I'd placed
Bones and skin
Together in a dream
You were put together that way
But I wouldn't let it go to my head if I were you

"My heart in pieces . . ."

My heart in pieces like the bits
Of traffic lost in the blue
Rain confused I roar off into
To learn how to build a ladder
With air in my lungs again
To be with you in that region
Of speed and altitude where our bodies
Sail off to be kissed and changed
By light that behaves like a hand
Picking us up in one state and putting
Us down in a different one every time

Now She Dwells Here

It was the work of fortune
which brings joy and not pain only.
But can a winged thing become less?

She lived on E. 75th Street
to speak plainly.

I mean: in the divisiveness of love
two people pass through
the same instant separately

for all their awareness sighs
for life and not for each other
but in doing that it does.

Things About You

1

I write this for your eyes and ears and heart
If it makes your eyes sore
                    ears weary
                    and heart burn
                    Stop!

                I come to things about you
        I didn't use to understand

I didn't mean to use you
                    I just summoned you

Then at the end you are soft and bent
The way a tulip is droopy a lilac is not

                    knowing this
            is a joyous experience
                    for me
        gives you endless pleasure

You are casual when others are only easy
You go directly toward your own thought
There are some things about you I don't understand

        that's why I married you

Do you think these are banal thoughts?

    that IS what it's all about
                the portrait for instance
    of the *inside* of the surface of something

The way *You Didn't Even Try* is "about"

Do out and in exist?

                                and up and down
                                are lies about them

        2

    Did you say something?

Up in Here

All her aroused feelings
  pour through a hole
      changing from particles to waves
      of noise to bury every signal

You chop your way out of the vocal bush
        using your cane for a pool cue
                    Now the shot
            the word pops into place
  bing!

You are passionate but afraid
          to fuse someone's mood
        the "you" that is asleep
        to the "she" that is you   a model
          of light and logic
                but you do

A pledge of allegiance to the mobility of the day
        where a bird lights on a branch
      like a beautiful song lighting on itself
            to bring you grace

One

Light spray over a daisy chain of days.
Many wives, brought on rocking boats,
Dissolve in one loved damsel.
Jury of sighs, it is Time
To load the back with groceries
With my brother and my wife
Because life is a family.
Did I drive right? Risky slopes
Deer start across, hushed timber
Cool and the engine smoking.
When mouths of fog cover the truck
Pushed by wind, the ocean sends
Us violet shrouds, bears
Brush us in the dark eucalyptus.
Where the hawk dives, a flowing zone
Lights the road. A brown head whispers
In the restless advance of trees
And cars, friends of lonesome men
In the brunt of a huge wave.

Ah—There

the emerald mosque
   in motion
      every time a fern

touches
   the honey
      colored comb

she pulls
   through her
     fallen hair

Pillow

Our arms sleep
Together under water

Air curves into the room
On feathers

Apple leaf light
Beneath the blanket

A butterfly of hair
In the breeze

Nimble Rays of Day
Bring Oxygen to Her Blood

After the sponge bath
Spice cake and coffee
In a sky blue china cup

Tiny clouds float by
Like bits of soap
In a bowl of very blue water

A happy baby sleeps
In a silky chamber
Of my wife's lovely body

A leaf spins itself
The leaf's a roof
Over the trembling flower

Everything's safe there
Because nothing that breathes
Air is alone in the world

Air

The sweet peas, pale diapers
Of pink and powder blue, are flags
Of a water color republic
The soft bed, turned back,
Is a dish to bathe in them.
This early in the morning
We are small birds, sweetly lying
In it. We have soft eyes,
Too soft to separate the parts
Of flowers from the water, or
The angels from their garments.

Every Day

You're sleeping with your hands
Between your legs
And your hair blown back
Across the pillow
Like a mane

The more times you sing to me
From the mare's smoothness
Inside your body cavity
The less lost I feel
When I walk past the dead people

Crisis on the Savannah

"I must complain the cards are
ill-shuffled till I have a good hand."

—Jonathan Swift

"Believing something will happen
  Because I don't want it to
And that some other thing won't
  Because I do—" I wailed to the dealer—

"This is desperation." "Yeah?" he said. But then by
  Your graceful lines, your lioness' mane,
Your heat as you returned from
  Your day in the jungle, you relieved me from

What in myself was desperate,
  What even now insists on wishing
And believing. Still in the sheen of finely-breathing
  Blond hair that covers you,

By the flashing way you move from tree
  To tree, and from room to room,
Making it a bright full house,
  I find at least the light to see the cards I am dealt.

Gift of Tongue

It's Christmas Eve and I run in the sun
There's not much holiday traffic on Mesa

A VW goes by with surf board sticking
Up through the roof like a shark fin
A girl on a black horse says "Hi!"

Christmas trees line the center of Brighton
Kids went to the city and got em
One of em's even covered with real snow

So goodbye to another year and I don't know
What to make of it though I'm fairly
Sure it won't be money
I'm pondering that seriously

When you come down the stairs in blue velvet
Like a long cool drink of water viewed
Through a prism of purest ultramarine
And all of a sudden I can speak English

Life Notes

Like a big tired buffalo
      or ox
Mount Tam kneels beneath
     a glittering ceiling
her blue and green
       flanks rest, her shaggy
head settles
     and drinks from the lagoon.
The fur of her underbelly is burnt and brown
cars wind down in it
      like ticks. The top
of her head is yellow and balding
except where a few squiggly redwood tips
crest it. She rests, in the blazing
light of a June afternoon, as I do.

Life is not conditional. IF
is only a
    half-life.
A Whole Life—yours, mine, its—
can pass by in an instant. Hers
continues, like a music without notes,
unless you really strain
your ears to hear them, and maybe even then.

Whistle Buoy

That grey droning note
  I've heard every dusk

Neither owl nor foghorn
  but similar to both

The low fluted "day-is-done"
  of some unknown warbler

Atonally breathy memo
  of universal mysterioso

Tucks misty roses away
  in the dark's soft envelope

Safe under a lion's paw
  of starry numerology

Whose silver figures
  fleck the surf's Afro

Otherwise sparkling brassily
  into the liquid air

The Door to the Forest

for Jim Carroll

Eric Dolphy can't wake up:
the green light's still burning
by the gate. Pine cones

when stepped on by
dogs or raccoons, click
gently, like bones

into the mist, which
smells like mint; the
sounds diminish it;

the white fire rose
through the dropper's eye
falls; and the rain remains.

Slow Life

1

Cinematic blossoming of love gasoline

2

Blue windows behind the stars
   and silver flashes moving across them
  like spotlights at movie premieres

long cool windshield wiper bars

3

the butterfly gently opens itself like a fist
     dividing into wings   and drifting off
       over the cube's puzzled head

Birds

Sky full of blue nothing toward which the Magi
Move, like dream people who are Walt Fraziers of the air . . .
Sometimes the moves they make amaze them
For they will never happen again, until the end of time; but
    there they are.

So shall I be like them? I don't think so . . . and yet to float
Above the rolling H_2O
On wings that express the mechanics of heaven
Like a beautiful golden monkey wrench
Expresses mechanics of earth . . . t'would be bueno

Crows

Like the shore's alternation of door   wave
Shoe   wave, the displaced and disturbed
Air replaces itself with more air as casually
As attention grants itself, and I observe
Two crows sew themselves onto the lace flag
Of that flying cloud, whose cosmetic grace
Adorning the Plain Jane face of the day
Pins them in an unlikely halo of pale light
After one blast of which they dance away,
Croaking shrilly as abandoned divas
Whose black scarves flap in the breeze
Over every home and panorama, dark precise
Signs washed up on the air to be noticed
Out of a continuous process of succession

Sky

The green world thinks the sun
Into one flower, then outraces
It to the sea in sunken pipes.
But twisting in sleep to poetry
The blood pumps its flares out
Of earth and scatters them. And
They become, when they shine on
Beauty to honor her, a part of
Her laconic azure, her façade.

Eos

Solar emeralds melt and blend
In a slow flash flow
Silver eucalyptus sails above
Waves of lavender
We rise at daybreak
Light opens its pure brooch
Far out over the ocean
A machine of perfect touch

"The sun shoots high . . ."

The sun shoots high out over
the ocean to the west and when
it goes down into the cold water
at night it lights up the under
sides of the cirro-cumulus clouds
with bands of pink that go
over into gold and rosy yellow
against the great deepening blue
Hollywood baroque glory
anticorona canopy out
of which a violet glow
of red light lifted through cobalt
heralds the green flash

The Greeks

Deep in the air the past appears
As unreal as air to the boy
Or the apple of the world
To a girl whose eyes are pale and mild
Her hair is probably not real gold
Only a very good imitation of the Greeks'
Like a map of that world of early days
Where woman lives on a scarlet cloud
While man in colorless blunt noon
Splashes up at the blue variables
That pass by on an airplane of words
Into the sky which distributes gifts of
Rain and light over our lives equally
Infinite gifts we are unable to behold

Magic Arrival No. 7

Not less because in purple I descend
The western day through what you called
The loneliest air did you arrive at what you are,
A unison of every fragrant thing yet brief
Like the perfection, after rain, of the color
Blue, its clear articulation in the air
When it and the sun suddenly come in the room together

The Tire

The story thread runs out through your hands
To many places indicating them as snags
You take the tire apart   Even so the process
Solves its own knots as it continues gingerly
To slip out of your hands   There is always
A looseness open and moving it says here
In the event   Then why does every tug on the
Strings complicate everything ravelling
Up further the almost impossible ball   When
Know-how shows itself for what it is will Grace
Grow free and exact to award the useless
Virtues their place   Do I have to wrestle
With every thought on earth like this   I mean
Will an angel arrive and untangle them all

from **Suite**

Got to be there, so that she'll know
when she's with me she's home. On
the air waves across the nation
energy imagines it can move that way.
But sleep hides her modes as nature's.
Her skin is a dreaming surface—
blood drifts up through shadows,
light shifts on minimal rubies,
the spots on water where fish breathe . . .
impossible to see them coldly
or in some numerical epitome.

What the picture tells me is itself
Now I know how to go on:
hold still, dry your eyes.
Life is actual, warm and near
and completely without character
except for the melodious enigma
of her body and the possibility
of monkeying around with it immediately.
Otherwise, the room contains only
a metal writing table, a chair
a flower box, and *The Corpse* of Balthus.

The tones of voice are petty
for a while, then change to affection
then quiet is disclosed like
a jaguar running on damp grass
and the heartfalls converge for an
instant at speechless thunder now.
Neither knows whose limbs are whose,
or whether they are those of automata.
For a moment the ocean reaches in the window
and painlessly strangles consciousness
with a sheer cloth—a pair of ladies' hose?

☆

Then again by day fog drapes the boats
off, blocks the bouquet of the sea
wind, and creates vertical cathedrals.
The muscles turn to slop
or the extension of something electrical.
Then the chemical thing stops
happening. Anger's the logical product.
It explodes softly in heroic attitudes.
Breakfast looks black and your thumb hurts.
The clouds are scratched and used.
The pump isn't working. The purple
light spins around and around, very slowly.

☆

I draw a head. You ask
"who's that supposed to be?"
I won't tell you. We laugh
and fall back on the mattress
that's covered with pretty yellow cloth
and out the river flows, out the window
past the railroad and the town,

and the pine forest of this pillow
where there are light brown
beds of moist pine needles
touched by rays of sun.

☆

Her voice is heard, and then the child's
who is her daughter, and they both sound
very young, they are both young girls
and they are talking in the garden
under the pear trellis, and their
hair shines in the sun, and the pear
petals snow on them, and they are one
person, going down through linear
time, but apart from it, parallel
and talking, and breathing again
and flashing and moving along that line

☆

Warm ripe days. The sun floods the ridge with color
before dawn, slowly the reddish light implodes
and before dusk the moon floats up like a softball
over the sea. Starbright glimmers the weather
satellite in a position akin to that of Venus
or is it the skylab people coming down? Mutual
interests unite people on earth and in the sky,
ah and the heart sighs to be so satisfied
it beats against the skin to bespeak love's beauty
and the air brushes past it with a smoothness
borne by zephyrs from somewhere inland like Houston, Tex.
where the days are hard but the nights are long and warm
from various small fires static electricity causes
to crackle in the sheets, and draw up our auras.

☆

Thought is surrounded by a halo
glowing oddly green. Midsummer love
has aphonies, tuned in from zero.
The sheets are crumpled on the bed.
The skin is everywhere and drips.
The skeleton has gone on vacation.
You can hear birds sing in the woods
and the reef is clothed with sable.
A stray diamond may pivot on your neck,
or your knee be grazed by lips;
in the next room, a distant ball game
on the radio.

Radio

Don't hurt the radio for
Against all
Solid testimony machines
Have feelings
Too

Brush past it lightly
With a fine regard
For allowing its molecules
To remain 100% intact

Machines can think like Wittgenstein
And the radio's a machine
Thinking softly to itself
Of the Midnight Flower
As her tawny parts unfold

In slow motion the boat
Rocks on the ocean
As her tawny parts unfold

The radio does something mental
To itself singingly
As her tawny parts unfold
Inside its wires
And steal away its heart

Two minutes after eleven
The color dream communicates itself
The ink falls on the paper as if magically
The scalp falls away
A pain is felt
Deep in the radio

I take out my larynx and put it on the blue chair
And do my dance for the radio
It's my dance in which I kneel in front of the radio
And while remaining motionless elsewise
Force my eyeballs to come as close together as possible
While uttering a horrible and foreign word
Which I cannot repeat to you without now removing my
    larynx
And placing it on the blue chair

The blue chair isn't here
So I can't do that trick at the present time

The radio is thinking a few licks of its own
Pianistic thoughts attuned to tomorrow's grammar
Beautiful spas of seltzery coition
Plucked notes like sandpaper attacked by Woody
    Woodpecker

The radio says Edwardian farmers from Minnesota march
    on the Mafia
Armed with millions of radioactive poker chips

The radio fears foul play
It turns impersonal
A piggy bank was smashed
A victim was found naked
Radio how can you tell me this
In such a chipper tone

Your structure of voices is a friend
The best kind
The kind one can turn on or off
Whenever one wants to
But that is wrong I know
For you *will intensely to continue*
And in a deeper way
You do

Hours go by
And I watch you
As you diligently apply
A series of audible frequencies
To tiny receptors
Located inside my cranium
Resulting in much pleasure for someone
Who looks like me
Although he is seated about two inches to my left
And the both of us
Are listening to your every word
With a weird misapprehension
It's the last of the tenth
And Harmon Killebrew is up
With a man aboard

He blasts a game-winning home run
The 559th of his career
But no one cares
Because the broadcast is studio-monitored for taping
To be replayed in 212 years

Heaven must be like this, radio
To not care about anything
Because it's all being taped for replay much later

Heaven must be like this
For as her tawny parts unfold
The small lights swim roseate
As if of sepals were the tarp made
As it is invisibly unrolled
And sundown gasps its old Ray Charles 45 of *Georgia*
Only through your voice

A Difference

Something fallen out of the air, some
thing that was breathing there before
stopped: or say it is a difference

felt quickly on turning from one's work
to the window, and seeing there the same
trees the same color, the sky still without clouds,

changed only in reference to the trees
which also seem to have turned away.
The world still external but less distinct

at its center. For a few
seconds. Fall. The centerfielder drifts under
the last fly ball of the summer, and puts it away.

Baseball and Classicism

Every day I peruse the box scores for hours
Sometimes I wonder why I do it
Since I am not going to take a test on it
And no one is going to give me money

The pleasure's something like that of codes
Of deciphering an ancient alphabet say
So as brightly to picturize Eurydice
In the Elysian Fields on her perfect day

The day she went 5 for 5 against Vic Raschi

Clemente (1934–1972)

won't forget
his nervous
habit of
rearing his
head back
on his neck
like a
proud horse

The Color of Stepped on Gum

is the color of our times.
The light of our times is
the light in the 14th St.
subway at 2 a.m. The air
of our times is the air of the
Greyhound depot, Market
& Sixth. It is prime time. A passed
out sailor sits pitched
forward like a sack of laundry
in a plastic bucket seat
his forehead resting on
the movie of the week. *The Long Goodbye.*

Realism

The smashed weirdness of the raving cadenzas of God
Takes over all of a sudden
In our time. It speaks through the voices of talk show moderators.

It tells us in a ringing anthem, like heavenly hosts uplifted,
That the rhapsody of the pastoral is out to lunch.
We can take it from there.

We can take it to Easy Street.
But when things get tough on Easy Street
What then? Is it time for realism?

And who are these guys on the bus
Who glide in golden hats past us
On their way to Kansas City?

The Song of the Drowned Ghost in the Pool

The song of the drowned ghost in the pool's
heard like an admission that the soul's
three thousand years bereft in us, as a slow

settling like snowflakes in a paperweight
somebody dropped that long a time ago
of these crystals through the gene,

pearly drifts of the first stuff which drove
space craft out to range across the gates and
reaches of solar systems, seeds and puffballs

of eternity. The song drifts and echoes down
through the still translucent glass-
like water, as a helmsman compels the planet's never-

stopping forward path toward the outer
lights that glint and twinkle like some far Las
Vegas seen across the desert at night on flashing

pari-mutuel boards of creation.

The Blue Dress

I close my eyes
and see you at the age of 30
beyond the mist of affect
in your blue dress
so slim and viennese
in the sharon's picture gallery
at tissa's party
on a stormy night in 1974
with the ocean roaring
against the breakwater
I find you there with
all my projections
withdrawn at last
and what appears is
you in your blue dress
in the real objective secret
of your self
and the total beauty of your self
in your blue dress
which comes from forgotten existence
thickets of the 19th century
whose density disappears in
the evaporation of this thought
but nature never dies in time
because it never really existed
outside this recurrent bewildering
intensified mind ignition garden
we call creation

Final Farewell

Great moment in *Blade Runner* where Roy
Batty is expiring, and talks about how everything
he's seen will die with him—
ships on fire off the shoulder of Orion
sea-beams glittering before the Tannhauser gates.

Memory is like molten gold
    burning its way through the skin
It stops there.
                      There is no transfer
Nothing I have seen
will be remembered
beyond me
That merciful cleaning
of the windows of creation
will be an excellent thing
my interests notwithstanding.

But then again I've never been
    near Orion, or the Tannhauser
gates,

I've only been here.

Printed March 1992 in Santa Barbara & Ann
Arbor for the Black Sparrow Press by Graham
Macintosh & Edwards Brothers Inc. Text set in
Zapf by Words Worth. Design by Barbara Martin.
This edition is published in paper wrappers;
there are 200 hardcover trade copies;
125 hardcover copies have been numbered
& signed by the author; & 26 lettered copies have
been handbound in boards by Earle Gray, each with
an original drawing by Tom Clark.

Tom Clark's books include many volumes of poetry, from *Stones* (1969) and *Air* (1970) to five volumes of selected poems from Black Sparrow, *When Things Get Tough on Easy Street* (1978), *Paradise Resisted* (1984), *Disordered Ideas* (1987), *Fractured Karma* (1990) and *Sleepwalker's Fate* (1992). He is also the author of novels (*Who Is Sylvia?*, *The Exile of Céline*), literary essays (*The Poetry Beat: Reviewing the Eighties*), and biographies (*The World of Damon Runyon, Jack Kerouac, Late Returns: A Memoir of Ted Berrigan*, and *Charles Olson: The Allegory of A Poet's Life*).